PIANO · VOCAL · GUITAR

THE HISTORY OF ROCK

THE EARL'

0 0001 6713408 9

TRAILS WEST

FROM BOY BANDS TO WOMEN WHO ROCK
FROM R&B TO ALTERNATIVE ROCK
FROM POWER BALLADS TO GRUNGE

THE HISTORY OF ROCK – THE EARLY '90s, PAGE 4
'90s MUSIC & CULTURE GLOSSARY, PAGE 14

This publication is not for sale in the EU.

ISBN 0-634-04551-2

HAL•LEONARD®
CORPORATION

7777 W. BLUEMOUND RD. P.O. BOX 13819 MILWAUKEE, WI 53213

SEP 23 2003

Visit Hal Leonard Online at
www.halleonard.com

CHRONOLOGICAL CONTENTS

CHART POSITION	DATE	TITLE	RECORDING ARTIST	PAGE
#1	1/20/90	How Am I Supposed to Live Without You	Michael Bolton	80
#3	3/31/90	I Wish It Would Rain	Phil Collins	105
#21	5/5/90	The Heart of the Matter	Don Henley	62
#3	5/5/90	How Can We Be Lovers	Michael Bolton	86
#33	5/19/90	Save Me	Fleetwood Mac	196
#1	6/9/90	Hold On	Wilson Phillips	75
#1	9/29/90	(Can't Live Without Your) Love and Affection	Nelson	154
#1	10/20/90	I Don't Have the Heart	James Ingram	96
#2	12/15/90	From a Distance	Bette Midler	54
#43	1/5/91	You Gotta Love Someone	Elton John	225
#4	5/18/91	I Touch Myself	Divinyls	100
#9	6/1/91	Silent Lucidity	Queensrÿche	212
#1	6/8/91	More Than Words	Extreme	172
#1	7/27/91	(Everything I Do) I Do It for You	Bryan Adams	91
#2	7/27/91	Right Here, Right Now	Jesus Jones	185
#26	8/17/91	Hard to Handle	The Black Crowes	59
#5	9/28/91	Love of a Lifetime	Firehouse	147
#1	10/12/91	Emotions	Mariah Carey	44
#6	1/11/92	Smells Like Teen Spirit	Nirvana	201
#1	1/25/92	All 4 Love	Color Me Badd	16
#1	2/29/92	To Be with You	Mr. Big	230
#1	3/21/92	Save the Best for Last	Vanessa Williams	206
#2	3/28/92	Tears in Heaven	Eric Clapton	220
#1	8/15/92	End of the Road	Boyz II Men	50
#6	8/22/92	Life Is a Highway	Tom Cochrane	140
#7	4/10/93	Two Princes	Spin Doctors	236
#17	5/1/93	If I Ever Lose My Faith in You	Sting	134
#31	7/17/93	Run to You	Whitney Houston	190
#1	9/11/93	Dreamlover	Mariah Carey	38
#20	10/30/93	No Rain	Blind Melon	178
#1	11/6/93	I'd Do Anything for Love (But I Won't Do That)	Meat Loaf	110
#3	1/22/94	Breathe Again	Toni Braxton	30
#5	5/14/94	Mr. Jones	Counting Crows	162
#2	5/28/94	I'll Remember	Madonna	124
#4	8/6/94	Can You Feel the Love Tonight	Elton John	34
#1	8/27/94	I'll Make Love to You	Boyz II Men	119
#4	9/10/94	When Can I See You	Babyface	242
#2	10/8/94	All I Wanna Do	Sheryl Crow	22
#8	1/21/95	I'm the Only One	Melissa Etheridge	128
#10	2/18/95	Hold My Hand	Hootie & The Blowfish	68

ALPHABETICAL CONTENTS

PAGE	TITLE	RECORDING ARTIST
16	All 4 Love	Color Me Badd
22	All I Wanna Do	Sheryl Crow
30	Breathe Again	Toni Braxton
34	Can You Feel the Love Tonight	Elton John
38	Dreamlover	Mariah Carey
44	Emotions	Mariah Carey
50	End of the Road	Boyz II Men
54	From a Distance	Bette Midler
59	Hard to Handle	The Black Crowes
62	The Heart of the Matter	Don Henley
68	Hold My Hand	Hootie & The Blowfish
75	Hold On	Wilson Phillips
80	How Am I Supposed to Live Without You	Michael Bolton
86	How Can We Be Lovers	Michael Bolton
91	(Everything I Do) I Do It for You	Bryan Adams
96	I Don't Have the Heart	James Ingram
100	I Touch Myself	Divinyls
105	I Wish It Would Rain	Phil Collins
110	I'd Do Anything for Love (But I Won't Do That)	Meat Loaf
119	I'll Make Love to You	Boyz II Men
124	I'll Remember	Madonna
128	I'm the Only One	Melissa Etheridge
134	If I Ever Lose My Faith in You	Sting
140	Life Is a Highway	Tom Cochrane
154	(Can't Live Without Your) Love and Affection	Nelson
147	Love of a Lifetime	Firehouse
162	Mr. Jones	Counting Crows
172	More Than Words	Extreme
178	No Rain	Blind Melon
185	Right Here, Right Now	Jesus Jones
190	Run to You	Whitney Houston
196	Save Me	Fleetwood Mac
206	Save the Best for Last	Vanessa Williams
212	Silent Lucidity	Queensrÿche
201	Smells Like Teen Spirit	Nirvana
220	Tears in Heaven	Eric Clapton
230	To Be with You	Mr. Big
236	Two Princes	Spin Doctors
242	When Can I See You	Babyface
225	You Gotta Love Someone	Elton John

THE EARLY '90s

**FROM BOY BANDS TO WOMEN WHO ROCK
FROM R&B TO ALTERNATIVE ROCK
FROM POWER BALLADS TO GRUNGE**

Ever since Little Richard unleashed "Tutti Frutti" and Elvis Presley graced the television shaking his booty, rock 'n' roll has been the music of the masses. Influencing economy, pop culture, and even politics, the form—through all of its incarnations and classifications—has nevertheless been a steadfast voice for youth, and now, for music lovers of all ages.

But just what *is* rock 'n' roll? At its birth, it was loud. It was promiscuous. It offered a sense of rebellion against mores of a generation past. Today, it's still loud, promiscuous, and offers a sense of rebellion against mores of a generation past. But it's also so much more. One look at the song list in this book speaks volumes about how encompassing the term "rock" has become over the last fifty years. Since the 1950s, its definition has expanded to include everything from pop, alternative rock and adult contemporary to heavy metal, rap-rock and grunge.

The decade of the 1990s—as every decade before and almost certainly every decade to come—had its own defining sounds across the genres. In the early 1990s, that defining sound was born in the Pacific Northwest with the emergence of grunge music, supplanting the hairspray-fueled cotton candy that hard rock had become. But other genres grew and evolved as well. The boy band seeds planted by New Kids on the Block and New Edition in the 1980s began to sprout. Eighties pop and R&B grew up with its listeners going from frat party soundtracks to cocktail party easy listening. The makeup, spandex and big hair of glam metal slowly de-accessorized to blue jeans, T-shirts and cropped coifs. And dinosaurs of the '60s, '70s and '80s continued to leave their imprints in the landscape of rock 'n' roll.

COLOR ME BADD

REBIRTH OF THE BOY BAND

What was the first boy band? One could argue that those four mop-topped Liverpool lads qualify based on the bubble-gum nature of their early work. Yes, The Beatles' "I Want to Hold Your Hand" could credibly be called the "I Want It That Way" of its day. Fortunately, as John, Paul, George and Ringo matured, their music followed suit, and the world was treated to the greatest rock band in history. Not long after, the Monkees hit television and radio airwaves. Then there were the Osmonds and the Jackson 5 in the '70s. In the '80s, New Kids on the Block and New Edition again prompted screams of adoration from legions of teen girls.

The early '90s saw two groups carry the boy band torch for a new generation. New York's Color Me Badd was first heard on the soundtrack for *New Jack City* with their hit R&B single, "I Wanna Sex You Up." That song was subsequently included on the quartet's debut album, the triple platinum-selling *C.M.B.*, which produced two more #1 hits in "I Adore Mi Amor" and "All 4 Love." So big was 1992 for this rather pedestrian foursome that only contemporaries Boyz II Men sat higher on the top pop singles charts. The future would not bode so well for Color Me Badd, however, as subsequent albums failed to capture the hearts or pocketbooks of the pop and R&B audiences. C.M.B. disbanded in the late 1990s.

Boyz II Men, a group of young men from Philadelphia infinitely more talented than their New York counterparts, cracked the charts with the irresistible, dance-inducing "Motownphilly" from their landmark debut, *Cooleyhighharmony*. They followed with the first of what would become a signature sound for the quartet: a chart-topping soulful ballad titled "End of the Road," which broke the record formerly held by Elvis Presley for most weeks spent at #1. After releasing a multi-platinum Christmas album in 1993, the Boyz followed the old adage, "If it ain't broke, don't fix it," on their sophomore effort, *II*, spawning the equally huge ballad, "I'll Make Love to You."

With the table set in the early '90s by Color Me Badd and Boyz II Men, new pretty faces would feast on the impressionable hearts of young teen girls and the wallets of their accommodating parents. Seminal boy acts Backstreet Boys and 'N Sync would become the biggest selling boy bands in history during the late '90s into the early 21st century.

HAIR METAL GETS A HAIRCUT

There is no doubt that rock in the '80s largely comprised new wave and glam rock. Affectionately referred to now as "hair metal," the bands in this category—the likes of Mötley Crüe, Poison, and Ratt—may have spent as much on clothing and hairspray as they did on musical instruments. And like any hot new thing, everybody wanted a piece of the action. Riding the coattails of the aforementioned pioneers were bands such as Nelson, Firehouse, Extreme, and Mr. Big.

Nelson was composed of the twin sons (Gunnar and Matthew) of '50s teen idol Ricky Nelson. Though they've maintained a recording career over the past 10 years, they are best known for their 1990 debut *After the Rain*, which included the megahits "(Can't Live Without Your) Love and Affection" and the equally sugary title track. Though critics panned the pretty duo because of their feminine looks and lack of a "bad boy" image, "Love and Affection" went all the way to #1, proving once again that fans know a good hook when they hear one.

NELSON

Extreme, a pop metal quartet who built their reputation on funk, groove, and the prodigious guitar chops of Nuno Bettencourt, captured their only #1 hit with a surprising acoustic duet titled "More Than Words." Taking advantage of the nascent unplugged phenomenon, the harmonious voices of Bettencourt and singer Gary Cherone brought Extreme to the mainstream.

A supergroup of sorts, Mr. Big featured the virtuosic talents of guitarist Paul Gilbert, bassist Billy Sheehan and drummer Pat Torpey, all led by the melodic rock scratch of vocalist Eric Martin. For a collection of musicians best known for their technical proficiency, as a group they realized the value of melody and well-written songs. After a debut record that was well-received among musicians, they resolved to go with the hook on their sophomore effort, 1991's *Lean Into It*. As with

their contemporaries in Extreme, the acoustic power ballad proved supreme, as "To Be with You" soared up the charts to #1 in early 1992. A second ballad, "Just Take My Heart," also did well; but after this, the band never quite reached the same acclaim.

Perhaps the most befitting of the hair metal title, Firehouse cashed in on the strength of two Top 20 hits, "Don't Treat Me Bad" and "Love of a Lifetime." The latter would eventually become one of the most popular wedding songs in recent memory, as countless couples danced their first steps as "Mr. and Mrs." to this power ballad of eternal, enduring devotion.

Often lumped into, but not truly deserving of the hair metal connotation was Queensrÿche, the so-called "thinking man's metal band." Shunning the "baby, baby" lyrics of their metal contemporaries, this Seattle-based quintet built a faithful underground progressive metal following with their seminal 1988 concept album *Operation: Mindcrime*, cementing their status as the premier prog rockers of their generation. They followed this epic tale of mind control, dirty politicians, religious hypocrisy and the human condition with the more accessible and commercially more successful *Empire* in 1990. The record sold over two million copies, largely on the popularity of the art-rock ballad "Silent Lucidity."

WOMEN WHO ROCK

If the '80s were dominated by dudes who looked like ladies, the early '90s saw real ladies take over the helm. Foreshadowing the incredibly successful Lilith Fair in the mid '90s, women in music provided a softer alternative to the grunge sound emerging early in the decade.

The modern queen mum of women who rock is without a doubt the marketing machine known as Madonna. Reinventing herself so often that even Darwin would wonder how she does it, the Material Girl has continually topped the charts, beginning with her 1984 hit, "Holiday," right through to her 2000 club hit, "Music." Her chameleon-like artistry and confident, unflinching business sense has made Madonna not only the most powerful woman in music history but arguably the most powerful artist, period.

Like Nelson, family ties ran thick in the pop vocal trio Wilson Phillips. Sisters Carnie and Wendy Wilson (daughters of Beach Boy Brian Wilson) and Chynna Phillips (daughter of John and Michelle Phillips of The Mamas & The

Papas) used their considerable genetic gifts to capture the airwaves in the summer of 1990 with the encouraging ditty "Hold On." Although these three ladies sold over four million copies of their self-titled debut, their 1992 follow-up, *Shadows and Light*, didn't fare nearly as well, and the band broke up the following year.

Melissa Etheridge's 1993 album, *Yes I Am*, put to rest not only the speculation about her lesbian lifestyle, but also whether the raspy, Janis Joplin–like singer would live up to her mounting potential. The record sold over six million copies on the strength of hits like "I'm the Only One" and "Come to My Window." That success was short-lived, however, as subsequent releases failed to capture the attention of rock audiences, and her much-advertised quest to have children with partner Julie Cypher via artificial insemination (fatherhood provided by David Crosby of all people) grabbed headlines.

If Melissa Etheridge was the hostess of the genre's "coming out" party, Sheryl Crow set the female singer-songwriter movement squarely on the path of continued success. In 1994, this lovely new face struck pay dirt with a million-dollar smile in the music video for her first single, "All I Wanna Do." Although Crow had previously toured the world with Michael Jackson and Don Henley, and had written songs for country queen Wynonna as well as pop diva Celine Dion, it was her quirky song about "matches and Buds and clean and dirty cars" that put her on the road to blue-collar divadom. "Leaving Las Vegas" and "Strong Enough" pushed her further into the spotlight, and after several more successful albums and singles in the '90s, Sheryl once again topped the charts with "Soak Up the Sun," arguably the biggest hit of Summer 2002.

POP TOPS THE CHARTS

Popular music, by definition, is not a genre, but rather music in any style that garners wide public adoration and acceptance. Yet somewhere along the line, the term "popular" was shortened to "pop," and it came to define acts combining elements of R&B and rock 'n' roll with an appeal to audiences not exclusive to any particular demographic. These artists— Bryan Adams, Bette Midler, Michael Bolton, Phil Collins, Hootie & The Blowfish, and many others like them—though often critically panned as safe and boring, regardless continue to create music that appeals to millions of fans around the world. And that, in short, *defines* popular music.

BRYAN ADAMS

In the early '80s, a young, raspy-voiced Canadian rocker named Bryan Adams found his way into the Top 10 with the ballad "Straight from the Heart" from his breakthrough record, *Cuts Like a Knife*. His follow-up, *Reckless*, spawned an amazing six Top 15 hits, including the youthful anthem, "Summer of '69," which had men from all across North America finding fond remembrance of their own "reckless" days. After the platinum-selling yet relatively disappointing *Into the Fire*, Adams scored his second #1 hit with "(Everything I Do) I Do It for You," the love theme from *Robin Hood: Prince of Thieves*. The song not only put Adams back on the musical map, but also became *the* Homecoming song of 1991.

If you were to look up "diva" in the dictionary, you'd almost certainly find a photo of Bette Midler. From her '60s Broadway debut in *Fiddler on the Roof* to her starring role in 1979's *The Rose* to her subsequent film, television and chart-topping appearances, "the divine Miss M." has captured the hearts and ears of millions of fans around the world. In 1989, Midler starred in *Beaches*, which featured "The Wind Beneath My Wings," an uplifting song that rejuvenated her slightly stalling career at the time. Riding that success, Midler released a comeback record titled *Some People's Lives* in late 1990. That record reached platinum status on the strength of the #2 single, "From a Distance."

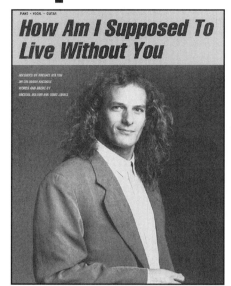

If ever there was a male "diva," you could argue it was the curly-haired former heavy metal singer, Michael Bolton. From rock star wannabe to contemporary crooner extraordinaire, Bolton found his voice on 1987's *The Hunger* with a soulful cover of the Otis Redding classic, "(Sittin' On) The Dock of the Bay." With this newfound formula for success, Bolton released *Soul Provider* in 1989. The record sold four million copies and spawned such classic power ballads as "How Can We Be Lovers" and "How Am I Supposed to Live Without You," the latter for which Bolton earned a Grammy for Best Male Pop Vocal Performance. Interestingly, this song, which Bolton co-penned, was a Top 40 hit for Laura Branigan in 1983.

As the drummer for pioneering progressive rockers Genesis beginning in 1970, Phil Collins probably never expected to become a popular, successful adult contemporary artist. Lacking the stereotypical rock star looks of fellow balladeer Bolton, the short, bald Brit-rocker Collins had to rely on sheer musical talent and a knack for writing hit songs. From Genesis, Collins made his first "revelation" as a solo artist with 1981's *Face Value*, which contained the haunting drum dirge of "In the Air Tonight." After several successful solo and Genesis ventures throughout the '80s, the diminutive drummer marched into the '90s with what may be his finest solo work, *But Seriously*. The record contained such hits as "Something Happened on the Way to Heaven" and the gospel-tinged "I Wish It Would Rain," which featured the legendary Eric Clapton on guitar.

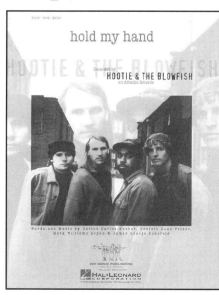

Ask Darius Rucker if there was one misconception about the enormously popular rock band Hootie & The Blowfish in the '90s, and he'll likely reply, "Yeah, my name's not Hootie!" In 1994, the University of South Carolina quartet began one of the most successful and steepest rises to the top in music history—followed by a nearly equally fast fall. The group's debut, *Cracked Rear View*, sold over 13 million copies in the U.S. alone with hits like "Let Her Cry," "Only Wanna Be with You" and "Hold My Hand," enticing sold-out crowds to continually chant, "Hoo-tie! Hoo-tie!" The group's 1996 release, *Fairweather Johnson*, although it sold over two million copies, was a relative flop, and both critics and fans alike decided it was time to blow off the fish.

GOT R&B?

Born out of the jump blues of the '40s, R&B has come to be associated with primarily African-American artists like Barry White, Aretha Franklin and Marvin Gaye. While those artists represent the old guard, artists such as Toni Braxton, Mariah Carey and Whitney Houston carried the torch of the soulful urban sound in the '80s and '90s. Though generally comprising minority artists, the R&B genre has had and continues to have tremendous crossover popularity, proving once again that a great song sung by a gifted voice can conquer any color lines.

James Ingram is a unique artist of the genre; while he has achieved enormous success with his numerous duets over the years, he has topped the charts only once as a solo artist. Working with such luminaries as Patti Austin ("Baby, Come to Me"), Michael McDonald ("Yah Mo B There") and Linda Ronstadt ("Somewhere Out There"), Ingram gained a reputation as a tremendous complementary voice. But it took 1990's #1 smash "I Don't Have the Heart" to show the music world once and for all that he could carry a tune all by himself.

JAMES INGRAM

For a while the heir apparent to Aretha Franklin, diva Whitney Houston hit the dance and R&B scene like a 20-megaton bomb in March 1985 with her self-titled debut. The record became the biggest-selling debut for a female artist in music history, topping 13 million in sales. Houston set another record as the first artist ever to have seven consecutive singles reach #1, including her remake of Dolly Parton's heart-rending "I Will Always Love You." From the soundtrack to *The Bodyguard*, that song became the biggest-selling single in rock history (later eclipsed by Elton John's "Candle in the Wind 1997") and, along with "I'm Every Woman" and "Run to You," helped the soundtrack top an astounding 16 million in sales.

A disciple of Houston, singer Mariah Carey was the best-selling artist of the '90s—no small feat. Often panned for her peculiar vanity quirks and failed acting career, her stunning five-octave voice is an undeniable force in the industry. The diminutive singer was reportedly "discovered" when her demo tape made it into the hands of Columbia Records chief Tommy Mottola, who gave it a listen in his limo and decided to give the young Carey a record deal. That, however, was just the beginning for the mogul and his newfound talent; in 1993, the couple was wed. By 1997 they had split, but if it had a devastating effect on Carey personally, it didn't show in her music. She again topped the charts that year, the next, and the one after that, just as she had in every year during the '90s.

No doubt pop star Vanessa Williams ran away with the talent portion in the 1983 Miss America pageant. The first African-American woman to win the U.S. crown (which she was later forced to renounce in light of nude photos the beauty queen had shot for *Penthouse* magazine), the stunning Miss Williams didn't let the scandal bring her down, as she pursued her first love, singing. In 1992, Vanessa topped the pop charts with the beautiful ballad, "Save the Best for Last," from her multi-platinum album *The Comfort Zone*. Williams extended that comfort zone in 1997 when she landed her first big screen Hollywood role opposite Arnold

SAVE THE BEST FOR LAST

VANESSA
WILLIAMS

Phil Galdston
Jon Lind

ORIGINAL SHEET MUSIC COVER

Schwarzenegger in *Eraser*. In 1999, she found fame in the sports world when she married Los Angeles Lakers basketball star Rick Fox.

When opera-trained singer Toni Braxton caught the ears of world-class producers Antonio "L.A." Reid and Babyface, it marked the beginning of a prosperous partnership. Braxton, who had grown up singing gospel music with her family, became the first woman to sign with Reid's and Babyface's LaFace Records and made her mark on the soundtrack to Eddie Murphy's hit film, *Boomerang*, which included a duet with producer Babyface on the track, "Give U My Heart." Her self-titled debut album was much anticipated, and in 1993 she made good on the expectations, selling over 8 million copies on the backs of three Top 10 singles: "You Mean the World to Me," "Another Sad Love Song," and "Breathe Again."

Kenny "Babyface" Edmonds is one of the most successful R&B producers in the genre's history, an artist who almost single-handedly rejuvenated the music form in the '90s. Having worked with a veritable "Who's Who" of R&B—Toni Braxton, Bobby Brown, Sheena Easton, Mariah Carey, Celine Dion, Whitney Houston, and many others—Babyface revived the smooth, classic, crooning R&B sound, providing much-needed crossover potential to capture the adult contemporary market. Although his career as a performing artist has typically taken a backseat to his songwriting and producing talents, Babyface nonetheless found success. His acoustic guitar-based #4 hit "When Can I See You" nabbed Babyface the singer his first Grammy for Best Male R&B Vocal Performance. Then, in 1996 he cemented his credentials as a crossover producer, winning a Grammy for Record of the Year for producing Eric Clapton's "Change the World."

BIRTH OF THE ALT-GENERATION

The '90s was the decade that saw so-called "alternative" music become mainstream; yet somehow, the genre retained the misnomer. Alternative rock had come to be defined largely by college bands like R.E.M. in the '80s. Stylistically similar, bands like Counting Crows, Jesus Jones, and the Divinyls nevertheless also followed R.E.M.'s and the B-52s' track record for sales success; thus they could hardly be considered "alternative" rock choices.

Led by sexy Australian singer Christina Amphlett, the Divinyls maintained a fairly long career largely under the radar. Formed in 1981, the band entered the radar by performing the soundtrack to a film called *Monkey Grip*. The single from that soundtrack, "Boys in a Town," featured Amphlett in a schoolgirl outfit filmed from below a metal grate, a provocative image that would stay with the singer for quite a long time. After moderate success with their 1988 single, "Pleasure and Pain" (yet another suggestive song), the Divinyls struck big with 1991's self-gratification anthem, "I Touch Myself," the video for which again featured the bound singer in fishnet stockings.

Forever destined for the one-hit wonder club with their huge 1991 hit, "Right Here, Right Now," Jesus Jones did provide a fleeting glimpse of the future. Mixing techno dance beats and samples with driving guitars, the formula didn't do much in the pop music world. Some ten years later, however, nü metal acts like P.O.D. and Linkin Park have taken that formula to the next level with great success.

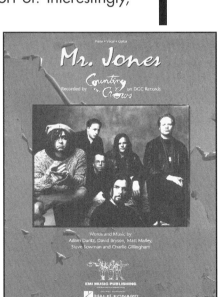

JESUS JONES

Caught somewhere between pop, classic rock and grunge, Blind Melon was an original band at a time when originality was a novel approach in music. Their early retro vibe and simple approach to songwriting held much promise, but it came to fruition only once, and that was in the form of their 1993 hit, "No Rain." Singer Shannon Hoon became yet another rock 'n' roll drug addiction statistic, and despite such coveted concert appearances as opening for Guns 'N Roses and The Rolling Stones, the band's career stalled. Hoon checked himself into rehab, but was unable to beat his addiction; he died of an overdose in October 1995.

The Spin Doctors were one of several hippie nouveau acts on the New York City scene in the early '90s, but their clever pop and blues-inflected songs helped them rise above the din and become an overnight success—well, sort of. Interestingly, their record *Pocket Full of Kryptonite* had been on record store shelves for over a year when radio and MTV picked up on the first single, "Little Miss Can't Be Wrong." Once the song and video made regular rotation, the fans ate it up. "Two Princes" followed, helping *Kryptonite* and the band reach multi-platinum prosperity.

ORIGINAL SHEET MUSIC COVER

Van Morrison was scheduled to play at the 1993 Rock and Roll Hall of Fame induction ceremony. When the hearty Irishman was a no-show, an unknown band called Counting Crows took the stage and won the hearts and ears of the star-studded audience. Later that year, the quintet released their debut record, *August and Everything After*—a somber, moody album featuring the morose lyrics and expressive vocals of dreadlocked frontman Adam Duritz. The group's first single, "Mr. Jones," bolted the band into the land of overnight success stories.

STILL ROCKIN'
AFTER ALL THESE YEARS

The early '90s certainly saw its share of successful new acts as well as several '80s holdovers, but even more impressive is the list of rock stars who got their start in the '60s and '70s. It's this longevity that each and every performing artist strives for, yet only a select few ever attain. Amazingly, many of these artists have not only overcome the changing tides of rock 'n' roll, but also drug and alcohol addiction and personal tragedy. To encapsulate each of their stories in

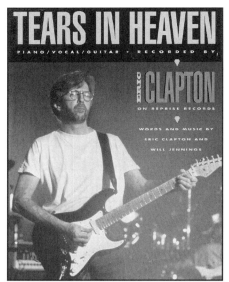

ORIGINAL SHEET
MUSIC COVER

these brief entries would be a miscarriage of journalistic justice. Even so, sometimes brevity is best.

At the top of this impressive list sits the legendary guitarist, Mr. Slow Hand himself, Eric Clapton. Starting with the Yardbirds, continuing with Cream and John Mayall's Blues Breakers, and finally hatching a solo career, Clapton's sweet guitar tone and mellifluous vocals have reached listeners for over 30 years now. Perhaps the most poignant performance of his illustrious career was the heartfelt ballad "Tears in Heaven," a song penned for his four-year-old son, who died tragically in a fall from a hotel balcony in March 1991.

In 1990, guitarist Lindsey Buckingham left his longtime mates in the venerable rock quintet, Fleetwood Mac. Wishing to forge ahead, the remaining members replaced Buckingham with two new members and released *Behind the Mask*. The record became the group's first since 1975 not to go gold. One highlight on the poorly received album, however, was the track "Save Me," which put the revamped band on the charts at #33. The classic Mac lineup of Stevie Nicks, John and Christine McVie,

ORIGINAL SONGBOOK
COVER FOR STING'S
TEN SUMMONER'S TALES

Mick Fleetwood, and Buckingham reunited temporarily to play President Bill Clinton's inauguration party in January 1993 with an unforgettable rendition of "Don't Stop," receiving a big thumbs up from the sax-playing Prez himself.

Sting has maintained not only his mass appeal through the years, but also seemingly his sex appeal, as year after year women name him one of the sexiest men in rock. While good looks certainly help in the image-conscious world of rock 'n' roll, it's not the only thing that counts (see Meat Loaf). The former Police frontman's mature, intellectual bent on songwriting attracts the adult contemporary crowd as well as his faithful college rock fan base. One highlight in Sting's career was his 1993 release, *Ten Summoner's Tales*, which contained the hit singles "If I Ever Lose My Faith in You" and "Fields of Gold." Part of his crossover appeal was made evident when the late Eva Cassidy covered the latter tune, and Olympic figure skater Michelle Kwan performed her routine to Eva's rendition of the ballad.

Other rockin' stars of the '70s topped the charts as well, interestingly, with love songs. Meat Loaf served up a man-size serving of balladry in 1993 with the biggest hit of his career, "I'd Do Anything for Love (But I Won't Do That)." Don Henley, one of the voices of the Eagles, cracked the Top 40 in 1990 with "The Heart of the Matter," just one of several ballads the drummer has recorded in the past decade.

ORIGINAL SHEET
MUSIC COVER

NIRVANA AT LAST

Last but not least, you cannot discuss rock music in the early '90s without giving major props to Kurt Cobain and Nirvana. Not since The Beatles and Jimi Hendrix had an artist changed the face of popular music like this Seattle trio. The band's commanding 1991 album, *Nevermind*—especially the first single, "Smells Like Teen Spirit"—bequeathed a sound as raw as the skin under a blister on an unsuspecting yet hungry rock audience. A direct result was the rise of the Seattle grunge sound and the new "anti-rock star" posturing of grunge bands—and later, post-punk and nü metal. On a societal level, Nirvana and bands influenced by their sound, approach, and attitude inspired disenfranchised teens to speak up and be heard, and helped spark a new Bohemian culture.

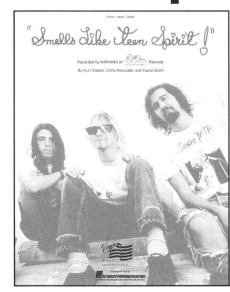

ORIGINAL SHEET MUSIC COVER

From the start, it was evident that the group, specifically Cobain, wasn't sure how to handle their newfound fame and attention. The singer/guitarist plunged into the dark world of drug abuse. He would later marry Hole singer Courtney Love; their relationship would result in a daughter. But even that was not enough to lure Cobain from the depths of heroin use. On April 5, 1994, Cobain took his own life with a self-inflicted gunshot wound to the head. Though the music world lost a bright star that tragic day, Cobain's momentary yet monumental influence still shines.

WHAT'S NEXT?

The answer is so simple, a sweat hog can figure it out. To quote Arnold Horshak's immortal words from the '70s television comedy, "Welcome Back, Kotter": "What is, is. What was, was. What will be *was*, but will be again." Music is an ever-changing landscape. It morphs, amalgamates, rebirths, and creates new sounds, fashions, and trends—year in, year out—impacting pop culture like nothing else. One thing we can be sure of, however, is that we ain't seen nothin' yet!

'90s MUSIC & CULTURE GLOSSARY

24/7: 24 hours a day, 7 days a week.

alternative (also, alt-rock): Guitar-based rock with disconnected male vocalists or chirpy female vocalists. It grew in response to the commercial success of bands such as R.E.M., Nirvana and Pearl Jam. Also known as modern rock.

AOL (America Online): Internet service provider that used an aggressive marketing campaign to become biggest ISP in the U.S. by the end of the decade.

bad hair day: When good hair goes bad. Usually the result of waking up late and not having time to properly style it.

"Beavis and Butthead": MTV hit cartoon about two teenage "burnouts," created by Mike Judge.

cappuccino: Popular Italian coffee drink resurrected by the Bohemian culture of the '90s.

chill: To simply hang out in one place for an extended period of time, usually a mall, bar, or someone's house, and usually with at least one other person.

coffee shop: Popular meeting place of '90s so-called intellectual Bohemian culture, whether to write poetry, conceive the plot of an indie film, or—like most people—simply to meet a friend for coffee.

crash: To spend the night at someone else's house, usually after a long night out.

da bomb: Refers to something being of excellent quality; the best.

diss: From rap culture, it is short for "dismiss" and means to rebuke or ignore somebody in a public manner, usually in front of friends.

dot-com: Slang for online business ventures.

e- (electronic): Similar to "cyber," it refers to real-life activities that took on new life on the Internet, such as e-mail, e-commerce, e-trading.

East Coast sound: Rap music style made popular by artists from the East Coast of the U.S. Artists include Biggie Smalls and Wu-Tang Clan.

fly: Attractive in a sexual way. ("Will there be any fly ladies at the party?")

gangsta rap: A form of rap music characterized by violent, often degrading lyrics.

Generation X: The generation of children born between 1965 and 1979 that followed the "baby boomers." Most commonly, the label refers to the grunge and alternative rock kids of the early '90s.

goatee: a beard in which facial hair is grown only around the mouth and chin area.

goth: A person whose wardrobe is nearly exclusively black and emulates vampire styles. Goths often have body piercings and tattoos, and listen primarily to industrial music such as Nine Inch Nails.

grunge: The label applied to a rock form featuring distorted guitars, whining vocals and flannel-shirt-wearing band members. Popularized by and associated primarily with Seattle bands such as Nirvana and Alice in Chains.

heavy metal: A ponderous rock form characterized by brittle, flashy guitar work, unnaturally high-pitched male vocals, and an adolescent fascination with the darker side of human experience. Born in the late 1960s of bands such as Black Sabbath and Led Zeppelin, heavy metal is currently associated with bands such as Metallica and Korn. Also called metal and speed metal.

hip-hop: The cultural context of rap music found in the urban style of dress, speech and art.

jazz: American music born in the early part of the century from African rhythms and slave chants. It developed from early ensemble improvisation to big band swing to the soloing brilliance of bop to thorny atonality and back to the current rearticulation of melody and harmony.

macarena: An audience participation dance originated in Spain by Los Del Rio.

mosh: The act of careening into other people at heavy metal concerts. Though the intention is non-injurious, bruises, sprains, cuts, and missing teeth are common.

mosh pit: The space at a heavy metal concert, usually near the front and center, where moshing takes place.

MP3: Abbreviation for MPEG Third Layer, an audio file compression method that converts recorded analog sound into a highly compressed (i.e., fast to download) digital format.

Napster: Internet file-sharing program used by music fans to share music catalogs online. Caused major debate between users and record labels as to what defines online theft.

new wave: An emotionally detached style of rock music characterized by a synthesized sound and a repetitive beat.

nü metal: An aggressive, generally up-tempo form of heavy metal characterized by thundering, downtuned guitar riffs, growling vocals, and a rebellious adolescent-based view of the darker side of human experience.

peace out: A modern take on the '60s anti-war salute, "Peace." Made popular by rap musicians in the '90s, "peace out" became an anti-violence salute for urban youth.

phat: Equivalent of "cool," it was first made popular in hip-hop circles. Usually refers to an inanimate object. ("Man, that stereo is phat!")

punk: A rock form characterized by aggressive volume, short, angry vocals and often bitter political or hopeless emotional content. Early exponents of punk include Sex Pistols, The Clash, Ramones, and Buzzcocks. Punk's recent revival is attributed to the dominance of sound-alike "alternative" bands.

rap: Urban, typically African-American music that features spoken lyrics, often reflecting current social or political issues, over a background of sampled sounds or scratched records.

rap-rock: A blend of rap and rock music made popular by artists like Limp Bizkit.

rave: Typically illegal, all-night parties fueled by prerecorded techno music and accompanying light show, usually in an abandoned building. The location is often undisclosed until the day of the rave.

R&B (Rhythm & Blues):
The all-encompassing term used to describe the African-American wellspring of postwar popular music. From rhythm & blues has come rock, soul, funk, rap, and regional and stylistic offshoots.

rock: Perhaps the most popular form of 20th-century music, a combination of African-American rhythms, urban blues, folk, and country music of the rural South. It has developed since the early 1950s into hundreds of sub-genres, each with its own audience, record labels, and radio formats.

Seattle: The largest city in the state of Washington, Seattle gained a popular identity as the cultural center of two major phenomena in the '90s: grunge rock and Starbucks coffee.

ska: Music combining reggae and punk rock sounds.

soul: The name for a type of rhythm & blues built on elements of gospel and spiritual music. Often, practitioners such as Sam Cooke maintained two careers simultaneously in soul and pop music.

"South Park": Animated television series by Trey Parker and Matt Stone featuring crude humor from the show's four 9-year-old characters: Stan, Kyle, Cartman, and Kenny.

Snapple: Flavored tea-based alternative to soft drinks.

Starbucks: Monster retail coffee chain born in Seattle, Washington's Pike Place Market as a high-quality, gourmet coffeehouse that set the template for branding and marketing in the '90s.

Sport Utility Vehicle (SUV): Trucks designed for urban transport made popular by post-college yuppies.

"The Simpsons": Cartoon sitcom by Matt Groening. The series, which has frequently featured cartoon musical guests such as Red Hot Chili Peppers, became the longest-running animated series in history.

techno: Dance music derived from disco, synth pop, and hip-hop, where the trancey, hypnotic beat is most important in the mix.

weak: Describes an action lacking in effort, thought, or coolness. ("That was weak of Jim to show up two hours late for band practice.")

West Coast sound: Rap music style made popular by artists residing on the West Coast of the U.S. Artists include Tupac Shakur and Snoop Dogg.

what-ever: An expression of disbelief, typically vocalized as two distinct syllables.

Woodstock: Music festival held in Woodstock, NY in 1994 and 1999, celebrating the 25th and 30th anniversaries, respectively, of the original festival in 1969.

World Wide Web: Electronic conduit of commerce, information and entertainment born in 1992.

X-Games: Based loosely on Olympic competition, the X-Games involve sports and music popular to the Gen-X demographic. This includes BMX biking, skateboarding and snowboarding.

ya think?: Spoken plainly, it is similar in function to the "really?" affirmation. With a more sarcastic tone, it serves as an affirmation when someone states the obvious.

yeah: Sarcastic affirmation made popular by characters on the "Friends" television series. It is typically vocalized as two syllables (y-eah), with the accent on the second syllable.

ALL 4 LOVE

Words and Music by ISAAC HAYES,
STEVE CROPPER, HOWARD THOMPSON,
BRYAN KYETH ABRAMS, MARK CALDERON,
SAM WATTERS and KEVIN KRAIG THORNTON

I'm so glad you're my girl, I'll do an-y-thing for you.
I will nev-er leave you, sug-ar, this I guar-an-tee. I

Call you ev-'ry night and give you flow-ers too. I
look in-to the fu-ture, I see you and me.

ALL I WANNA DO

Words and Music by KEVIN GILBERT,
DAVID BAERWALD, SHERYL CROW,
WYN COOPER and BILL BOTTRELL

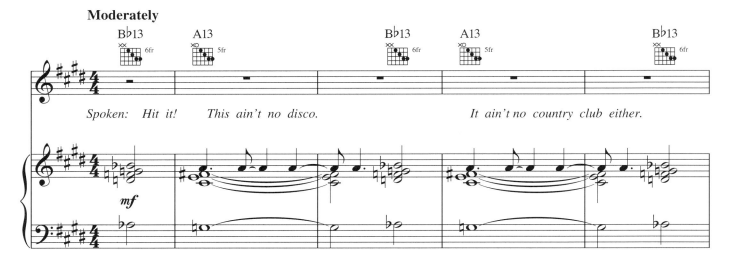

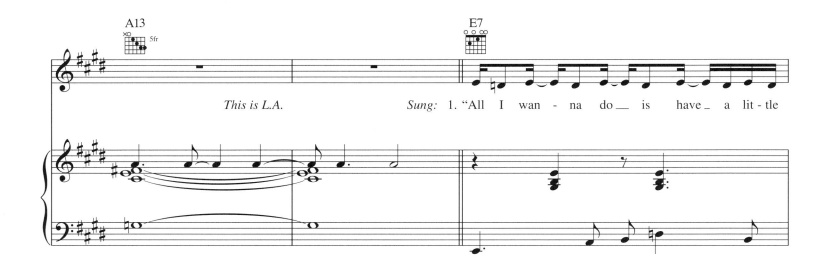

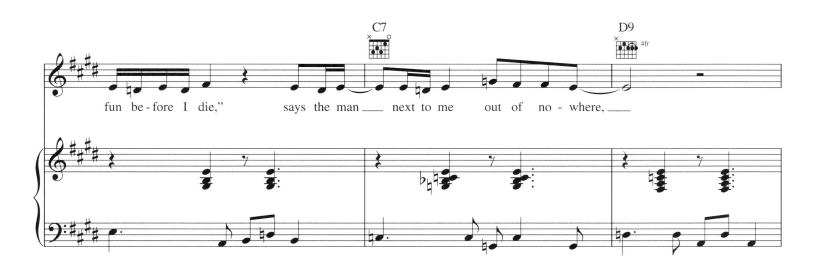

Additional Lyrics

3. I like a good beer buzz early in the morning,
   And Billy likes to peel the labels from his bottles of Bud
   And shred them on the bar.
   Then he lights every match in an oversized pack,
   Letting each one burn down to his thick fingers
   Before blowing and cursing them out.
   And he's watching the Buds as they spin on the floor.
   A happy couple enters the bar dancing dangerously close to one another.
   The bartender looks up from his want ads.

BREATHE AGAIN

Words and Music by
BABYFACE

Moderately slow

If I nev-er feel you in my arms a-gain, if I nev-er feel your ten-der kiss a-

gain, if I nev-er hear "I love you" now and then, will I

nev-er make love to you once a-gain? Please un-der-stand, if __ love __ ends, ___ then I

Can You Feel The Love Tonight

from Walt Disney Pictures' THE LION KING
As Performed by Elton John

Music by ELTON JOHN
Lyrics by TIM RICE

There's a calm ___ sur-ren-der
There's a time ___ for ev-'ry-one,

to the rush ___ of day, ___ when the heat ___ of the roll-ing world ___
if they on-ly learn ___ that the twist-ing ka-lei-do-scope ___

can be turned ___ a-way. ___ An en-chant-ed mo-ment,
moves us all ___ in turn. ___ There's a rhyme ___ and rea-son

DREAMLOVER

Words and Music by MARIAH CAREY
and DAVE HALL

EMOTIONS

Lyrics by MARIAH CAREY
Music by MARIAH CAREY, DAVID COLE and ROBERT CLIVILLES

END OF THE ROAD

from the Paramount Motion Picture BOOMERANG

Words and Music by BABYFACE,
L.A. REID and DARYL SIMMONS

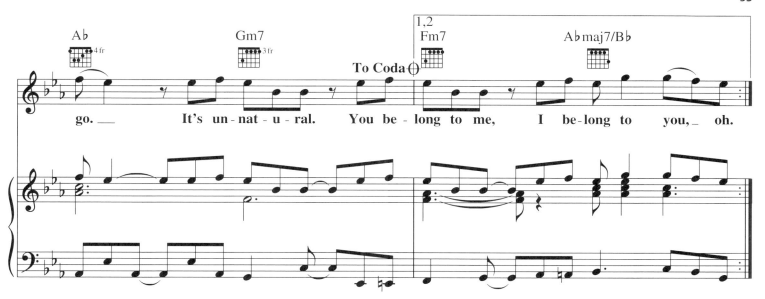

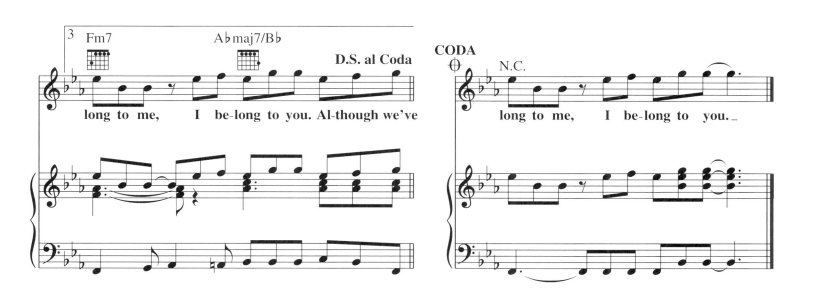

Additional Lyrics

(Spoken:) Girl, I'm here for you.
All those times at night when you just hurt me,
And just ran out with that other fellow,
Baby, I knew about it.
I just didn't care.
You just don't understand how much I love you, do you?
I'm here for you.
I'm not out to go out there and cheat all night just like you did, baby.
But that's alright, huh, I love you anyway.
And I'm still gonna be here for you 'til my dyin' day, baby.
Right now, I'm just in so much pain, baby.
'Cause you just won't come back to me, will you?
Just come back to me.

Yes, baby, my heart is lonely.
My heart hurts, baby, yes, I feel pain too.
Baby please...

FROM A DISTANCE

Words and Music by
JULIE GOLD

HARD TO HANDLE

Words and Music by ALLEN JONES,
ALVERTIS BELL and OTIS REDDING

1., 3. Ba - by, here I am, ___ I'm a man ___ on the scene. ___
2. Ac - tions speak loud-er than words, and I'm a man of great ex - per - ience.
4. *Instrumental*

I can give you what you want ___ but you got ___ to come home with me. ___
I know you got an - oth - er man, ___ but I can love you bet-ter than him. ___

I got ___ some good ___ old lov - in' and I've got some more in store. ___
Take my hand, don't be ___ a - fraid, ___ I want to prove ev - 'ry word I say. ___

Vocal ad lib. to end

THE HEART OF THE MATTER

Words and Music by JOHN DAVID SOUTHER,
DON HENLEY and MIKE CAMPBELL

Moderately slow

I got the call _ to- day, I didn't want to hear _ but I knew that it _ would come. _
(See additional lyrics)

An old, _ true friend of ours _ was talk- in' on _ the phone, _ she said you

and the ash - es will scat - ter. So, I'm think - in' a - bout for - give - ness,
for- give- ness,

for- give - ness   e - ven if, __ e - ven if __ you don't love __ me.

Additional Lyrics

Verse 2:   These times are so uncertain
There's a yearning undefined
... people filled with rage
We all need a little tenderness
How can love survive in such a graceless age?
The trust and self-assurance that lead to happiness
They're the very things we kill, I guess
Pride and competition
    cannot fill these empty arms
And the work I put between us
    doesn't keep me warm

Chorus 2:   I'm learning to live without you now
But I miss you, baby
The more I know, the less I understand
All the things I **thought** I'd figured out
I have to learn again
I've been trying to get down
    to the heart of the matter
But everything changes
    and my friends seem to scatter
But I think it's about forgiveness
Forgiveness
Even if, even if you don't love me anymore.

HOLD MY HAND

Words and Music by DARIUS CARLOS RUCKER, EVERETT DEAN FELBER,
MARK WILLIAM BRYAN and JAMES GEORGE SONEFELD

HOLD ON

Words and Music by CARNIE WILSON,
CHYNNA PHILLIPS and GLEN BALLARD

HOW AM I SUPPOSED TO LIVE WITHOUT YOU

Words and Music by MICHAEL BOLTON
and DOUG JAMES

I could hard-ly be-lieve____ it when I
I'm too proud for cry - ing, did - n't

heard the news____ to - day.____ I had to come____ and get it straight____ from you.
come here to break down.____ It's just a dream of mine____ is com - in' to __ an end.

They said you are leav - in' some-one's
And how can I blame____ you when I

HOW CAN WE BE LOVERS

Words and Music by DESMOND CHILD,
MICHAEL BOLTON and DIANE WARREN

(Everything I Do)
I DO IT FOR YOU

from the Motion Picture ROBIN HOOD: PRINCE OF THIEVES

Words and Music by BRYAN ADAMS,
ROBERT JOHN LANGE and MICHAEL KAMEN

I DON'T HAVE THE HEART

Words and Music by ALLAN RICH
and JUD FRIEDMAN

I TOUCH MYSELF

Words and Music by BILLY STEINBERG,
TOM KELLY, CHRISTINE AMPHLETT and MARK McENTEE

I WISH IT WOULD RAIN

Words and Music by
PHIL COLLINS

Moderately

You know I ne-ver meant to see you a - gain, ___ and I

See lyrics for verses 2 & 3 (𝄋)

on - ly passed by as a friend, ___

VERSE 2:
You said you didn't need me in your life,
Oh I guess you were right,
Ooh I never meant to cause you no pain,
But it looks like I did it again.

VERSE 3:
'Cos I know, I know I never meant to cause you no pain,
And I realise I let you down,
But I know in my heart of hearts,
I know I'm never gonna hold you again.

I'D DO ANYTHING FOR LOVE
(But I Won't Do That)

Words and Music by
JIM STEINMAN

I'LL MAKE LOVE TO YOU

Words and Music by
BABYFACE

Close your eyes, make a wish, and blow
lax, let's go slow. I ain't

an - y - thing. _ Girl, you need on - ly ask.
ev - er you ask me, you know I could do. } I'll make love to you like you

want me to and I'll hold you tight, ba - by, all through the night. I'll make

love to you when you want me to and I will not let go till you

tell me to. _____ Girl, re -

I'LL REMEMBER

from the film WITH HONORS

Words and Music by PATRICK LEONARD,
RICHARD PAGE and MADONNA

I'M THE ONLY ONE

Words and Music by
MELISSA ETHERIDGE

Steady Rock

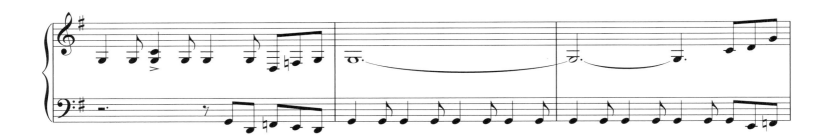

Please, ba - by, can't __ you see my
Please, ba - by, can't __ you see I'm

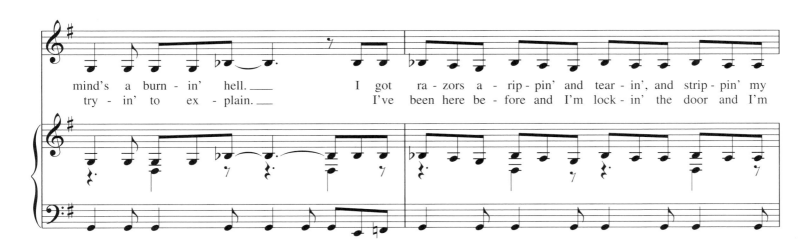

mind's a burn - in' hell. __ I got ra - zors a - rip - pin' and tear - in', and strip - pin' my
try - in' to ex - plain. __ I've been here be - fore and I'm lock - in' the door and I'm

de - mons that you're hid - in' from. ___ When all your prom - is - es ___ are gone, ___

___ I'm the on - ly ___ one. ___

only fear that makes you run, the de-mons that you're hid-in' from. When all your prom-is-es are gone, I'm the on-ly one.

Optional Ending

Repeat and Fade

Vocal ad lib.

IF I EVER LOSE MY FAITH IN YOU

Music and Lyrics by
STING

You could say I ___ lost ___ my faith in ___ sci-
Some would say I was ___ a lost ___ man in a ___ lost
I nev-er saw no mir-a-cle of sci-ence

-ence and prog-ress.
world.

LIFE IS A HIGHWAY

Words and Music by
TOM COCHRANE

Life's like a road_ that you trav-el on when there's one _ day here _ and the next_ day gone. Some-time
all these ci-ties and all these towns, it's in my blood_ and it's all _ a - round. _ I love

LOVE OF A LIFETIME

Words and Music by BILL LEVERTY
and CARL SNARE

153

(Can't Live Without Your)
LOVE AND AFFECTION

Words and Music by MARC TANNER,
MATT NELSON and GUNNAR NELSON

MR. JONES

Words by ADAM DURITZ
Music by ADAM DURITZ and DAVID BRYSON

MORE THAN WORDS

Words and Music by NUNO BETTENCOURT
and GARY CHERONE

Original key: F# major. This edition has been transposed up one half-step to be more playable.

NO RAIN

By BLIND MELON

All I can say ___ is that my life is pret-ty plain, ___ I

Play 4 times

Guitar solo - ad lib.

All I can say ___ is that my life is pret-ty plain, ___ you don't

like my point of view, ___ you think that I'm in - sane. It's ___ not

D.S. al Coda

sane, ___ it's ___ not sane. ___

RIGHT HERE, RIGHT NOW

Words and Music by
JESUS JONES

RUN TO YOU

from the film THE BODYGUARD

Words and Music by ALLAN RICH
and JUD FRIEDMAN

SAVE ME

Words and Music by CHRISTIE McVIE
and EDDY QUINTELA

Hey, __ you, _____ the one _____ with the laugh -
_____ you could _____ own the u -

(D.S.) Instrumental

- ing eyes, _____ you, _____ the one _____ with the haunt -
- ni - verse; _____ think _____ a - bout _____ it _____ and you'll re -

SMELLS LIKE TEEN SPIRIT

Words and Music by KURT COBAIN,
CHRIS NOVOSELIC and DAVID GROHL

Save the Best for Last

Words and Music by PHIL GALDSTON,
JON LIND and WENDY WALDMAN

SILENT LUCIDITY

Words and Music by
CHRIS DeGARMO

*1st time vocal is sung one octave lower than written.

(Spoken:) Visualize your dreams. Record it in the present tense. Put it into a permanent form.

If you persist in your efforts, you can achieve dream control...

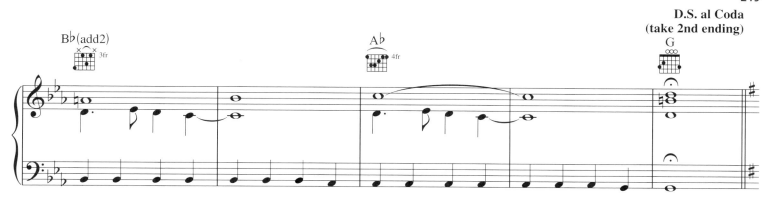

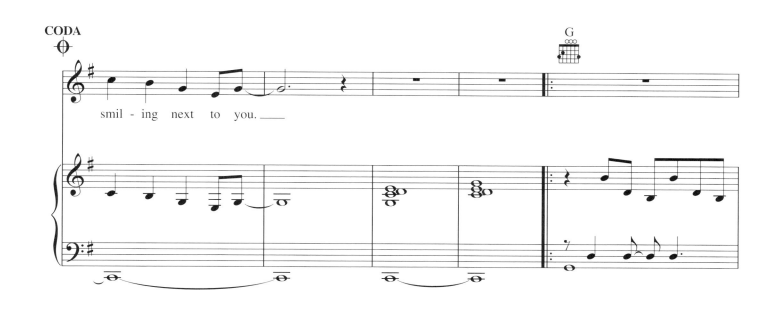

TEARS IN HEAVEN

Words and Music by ERIC CLAPTON
and WILL JENNINGS

Be-yond the door ___ there's peace, I'm sure, ___

YOU GOTTA LOVE SOMEONE

Words and Music by ELTON JOHN
and BERNIE TAUPIN

Guitar solo ends

TO BE WITH YOU

Words and Music by ERIC MARTIN
and DAVID GRAHAME

Why be a - lone __ when we can be to-geth - er, ba - by?

You can make __ my life __ worth - while. __ I can make __ you start to

smile. __

TWO PRINCES

Words and Music by
SPIN DOCTORS

Solo ends Said

WHEN CAN I SEE YOU

Words and Music by
BABYFACE

244

HISTORY OF ROCK

THE HISTORY OF ROCK: THE BIRTH OF ROCK AND ROLL

The first volume explores rock's rhythm and blues roots and its earliest tunes – from "Rocket '88" and "Shake, Rattle and Roll" to the major hits of Elvis Presley, Little Richard, Jerry Lee Lewis, Buddy Holly, and more. 37 songs, including: All Shook Up • Blueberry Hill • Blue Suede Shoes • Earth Angel • Heartbreak Hotel • Long Tall Sally • Lucille • Goodnight, It's Time to Go • The Green Door • Rock Around the Clock • Tutti-Frutti • and more! 136 pages.
00490216 Piano/Vocal/Guitar.................................$12.95

THE HISTORY OF ROCK: THE LATE '50S

The declaration "Rock and Roll Is Here to Stay" led the way for American Bandstand greats like Paul Anka, Frankie Avalon, Fabian, Bobby Darin, and Connie Francis. This book also explores the novelty song hits, the close harmony styles, and romantic ballads that filled the radio waves. 48 songs, including: At the Hop • Chantilly Lace • Do You Want to Dance? • Great Balls of Fire • Lollipop • Rock and Roll Is Here to Stay • Sea of Love • Splish Splash • Tears on My Pillow • Tequila • Wake Up, Little Susie • Yakety Yak • and more. 176 pages.
00490321 Piano/Vocal/Guitar.................................$14.95

THE HISTORY OF ROCK: THE EARLY '60S

Surf music, doo wop, and dance crazes set the stage for a new decade. This volume explores the success of the Beach Boys, "Big Girls Don't Cry," and the Twist. 56 songs, including: Barbara Ann • Breaking Up Is Hard to Do • Do Wah Diddy Diddy • Duke of Earl • Hit the Road, Jack • Louie, Louie • My Boyfriend's Back • Runaway • Sherry • Surfin' U.S.A. • Tell Laura I Love Her • The Twist • Under the Boardwalk • Wooly Bully • and more. 184 pages.
00490322 Piano/Vocal/Guitar.................................$15.95

THE HISTORY OF ROCK: THE MID '60S

The British invaded the charts and Hendrix re-invented the guitar in this volume, featuring chart toppers of the Beatles, the Moody Blues, the Hollies, Rolling Stones, Mamas and the Papas, James Brown, the Byrds, and many more. 49 songs, including: All Day and All of the Night • California Dreamin' • Can't Buy Me Love • Gloria • Groovin' • Help! • Hey Joe • I Want to Hold Your Hand • Wild Thing • Yesterday • and more. 200 pages.
00490581 Piano/Vocal/Guitar.................................$15.95

THE HISTORY OF ROCK: THE LATE '60S

The turbulence of this era created a new mood for rock and roll. From the classic "Sgt. Pepper's Lonely Hearts Club Band" to the San Francisco sound and Janis Joplin to the jazz/rock hits of Blood, Sweat and Tears, you'll find the songs that made the statements of the time in this volume. 47 songs, including: Born to Be Wild • Come Together • Hey Jude • San Francisco (Be Sure to Wear Some Flowers in Your Hair) • Spinning Wheel • The Sunshine of Your Love • White Room • A Whiter Shade of Pale. 190 pages.
00311505 Piano/Vocal/Guitar.................................$15.95

THE HISTORY OF ROCK: THE EARLY '70S

The Beatles broke up, Southern bands brought their brand of rock and roll to the top of the charts, heavy metal was just in its infancy, and "American Pie" glorified the day the music died. Cooper and Bowie made rock a spectacle while the Moody Blues made it an art. From Black Sabbath to Neil Diamond, David Bowie to Elton John, the early '70s were a breeding ground for music superstars still around today. Features 45 hits, including: American Pie • Fire and Rain • Imagine • Maggie May • Rikki Don't Lose That Number • Sweet Home Alabama • and more. 208 pages.
00311538 Piano/Vocal/Guitar.................................$15.95

THE HISTORY OF ROCK: THE LATE '70S

In the late '70s the piano men — Sedaka, John, and Joel — shared the charts with Kansas, Foreigner, and Aerosmith. Women fought for equality and won on the charts with Streisand, Tyler, Ronstadt and Gaynor on top. Underground grumblings of black leather punk began while the music of the Bee Gees and Donna Summer kept people in white satin dancing all night. 43 hits, including: Bad Case of Loving You • Bennie and the Jets • Dust in the Wind • Hot Blooded • I Will Survive • Piano Man • Walk This Way • and more. 208 pages.
00311603 Piano/Vocal/Guitar.................................$15.95

THE HISTORY OF ROCK: THE EARLY '80S

The last dregs of disco were cleaned off the charts by new wave, punk, contemporary hit radio, and heavy metal. The rock heavyweights — John Lennon, Paul McCartney, Stevie Wonder, Chicago, Billy Joel — shared the charts with slick newcomers — Human League, Culture Club, Eurythmics, Police — and the women of rock — Tina Turner, Joan Jett, Cyndi Lauper, Pat Benatar, and many more. 42 songs, including: Do You Really Want to Hurt Me • Every Breath You Take • I Love Rock 'N' Roll • Maniac • Owner of a Lonely Heart • Sweet Dreams (Are Made of This) • Total Eclipse of the Heart • What's Love Got to Do With It • Woman • and more. 256 pages.
00311619 Piano/Vocal/Guitar.................................$15.95

THE HISTORY OF ROCK: THE LATE '80S

Shut up and dance became the war cry of 80s rock as videos paved the way for glamorous new stars. There were New Kids on the Block, Paula Abdul, Madonna, Bobby Brown, Milli Vanilli, and those who had been around the block: Sting, Foreigner, Beach Boys, James Brown, and Robert Palmer. Mega-stars Michael Jackson, Madonna, Bon Jovi, and U2 shot to the top of the charts as rap started easing its way up to the mainstream. 43 songs, including: Addicted to Love • Careless Whisper • Hangin' Tough • If You Love Somebody Set Them Free • Kokomo • Livin' on a Prayer • My Prerogative • Red, Red Wine • Straight Up • We Didn't Start the Fire • You Give Love a Bad Name • and more. 264 pages.
00311620 Piano/Vocal/Guitar.................................$16.95

THE HISTORY OF ROCK: THE EARLY '90S

The early '90s saw a variety of songs fighting for the top spots every week, from R&B ballads from Whitney and Mariah to new releases from old favorites Sting and Meatloaf. But the pivotal point was when a little-known band from the Northwest hit the airwaves and video channels with "Smells Like Teen Spirit." After Nirvana, grunge became a household name and flannels were officially back in fashion. This book provides a sampling of over 40 of the top tunes of the era complete with a great essay on the trends and hits of the day. Songs include: All I Wanna Do • All 4 Love • Can You Feel the Love Tonight • Dreamlover • (Everything I Do) I Do It for You • From a Distance • Hard to Handle • Hold My Hand • How Am I Supposed to Live Without You • I'd Do Anything for Love (But I Won't Do That) • If I Ever Lose My Faith in You • More Than Words • Mr. Jones • Right Here, Right Now • Smells like Teen Spirit • Tears in Heaven • Two Princes • and more.
00310866 Piano/Vocal/Guitar.................................$15.95

THE HISTORY OF ROCK: THE LATE '90S

The late '90s brought new releases from old favorites like Clapton and Madonna and fresh faces appeared on the scene like Oasis, Jewel, and Chumbawamba. Swing swung back in fashion and Hanson brought pop back to the charts with "Mmm Bop." But one song sunk all the competition: "My Heart Will Go On" from *Titanic* provided the blockbuster the music world was waiting for. This collection provides 42 of the top hits from that time complete with an extensive summary of the bands and events that made those years special. Songs include: Barely Breathing • Beautiful Stranger • Change the World • Counting Blue Cars • Give Me One Reason • I Will Remember You • Iris • Jump, Jive An' Wail • MMM Bop • My Heart Will Go On (Love Theme from 'Titanic') • Semi-Charmed Life • Smooth • Torn • Tubthumping • Wonderwall • You Were Meant for Me • and more.
00310870 Piano/Vocal/Guitar.................................$15.95

FOR MORE INFORMATION, SEE YOUR LOCAL MUSIC DEALER,
OR WRITE TO:

HAL•LEONARD®
CORPORATION
7777 W. BLUEMOUND RD. P.O. BOX 13819 MILWAUKEE, WI 53213

Visit Hal Leonard Online at **www.halleonard.com**

Prices, contents and availability subject to change without notice.

0203

The Greatest Songs Ever Written

THE BEST EVER COLLECTION

ARRANGED FOR PIANO, VOICE AND GUITAR

150 of the Most Beautiful Songs Ever
150 ballads: Bewitched • (They Long to Be) Close to You • How Deep Is Your Love • I'll Be Seeing You • Unchained Melody • Yesterday • Young at Heart • more.
00360735...$22.95

The Best Big Band Songs Ever
Over 60 big band hits: Boogie Woogie Bugle Boy • Don't Get Around Much Anymore • In the Mood • Moonglow • Sentimental Journey • Who's Sorry Now • more.
00359129...$16.95

The Best Broadway Songs Ever
Over 70 songs in all! Includes: All I Ask of You • Bess, You Is My Woman • Climb Ev'ry Mountain • Comedy Tonight • If I Were a Rich Man • Ol' Man River • more!
00309155...$20.95

The Best Christmas Songs Ever
More than 60 holiday favorites: Frosty the Snow Man • A Holly Jolly Christmas • I'll Be Home for Christmas • Rudolph, The Red-Nosed Reindeer • Silver Bells • more.
00359130...$19.95

The Best Classic Rock Songs Ever
Over 60 hits: American Woman • Bang a Gong • Cold As Ice • Heartache Tonight • Rock and Roll All Nite • Smoke on the Water • Wonderful Tonight • and more.
00310800...$17.95

The Best Classical Music Ever
Over 80 of classical favorites: Ave Maria • Canon in D • Eine Kleine Nachtmusik • Für Elise • Lacrymosa • Ode to Joy • William Tell Overture • and many more.
00310674...$19.95

The Best Contemporary Christian Songs Ever
Over 70 favorites, including: Awesome God • El Shaddai • Friends • Jesus Freak • People Need the Lord • Place in This World • Serve the Lord • Thy Word • more.
00310558...$19.95

The Best Country Songs Ever
78 classic country hits, featuring: Always on My Mind • Crazy • Daddy Sang Bass • Forever and Ever, Amen • God Bless the U.S.A. • I Fall to Pieces • Stand By Your Man • Through the Years • and more.
00359135...$17.95

The Best Early Rock N Roll Songs Ever
Over 70 songs, including: Book of Love • Crying • Do Wah Diddy Diddy • Louie, Louie • Peggy Sue • Shout • Splish Splash • Stand By Me • Tequila • and more.
00310816...$17.95

The Best Easy Listening Songs Ever
75 mellow favorites: (They Long to Be) Close to You • Every Breath You Take • How Am I Supposed to Live Without You • Unchained Melody • more.
00359193...$18.95

The Best Gospel Songs Ever
80 gospel songs: Amazing Grace • Daddy Sang Bass • How Great Thou Art • I'll Fly Away • Just a Closer Walk with Thee • Just a Little Talk with Jesus • The Old Rugged Cross • Will the Circle Be Unbroken • more.
00310503...$19.95

The Best Hymns Ever
118 of the most loved hymns of all time: Abide with Me • Every Time I Feel the Spirit • He Leadeth Me • I Love to Tell the Story • The Old Rugged Cross • Were You There? • When I Survey the Wondrous Cross • and more.
00310774...$17.95

The Best Jazz Standards Ever
77 jazz hits: April in Paris • Don't Get Around Much Anymore • Love Is Here to Stay • Misty • Satin Doll • Unforgettable • When I Fall in Love • and more.
00311641...$18.95

The Best Latin Songs Ever
67 songs, including: Besame Mucho (Kiss Me Much) • Blame It on the Bossa Nova • The Girl from Ipanema • Malaguena • One Note Samba • Slightly Out of Tune (Desafinado) • Summer Samba (So Nice) • and more.
00310355...$19.95

The Best Love Songs Ever
65 favorite love songs, including: Endless Love • Here and Now • Love Takes Time • Misty • My Funny Valentine • So in Love • You Needed Me • Your Song.
00359198...$17.95

The Best Movie Songs Ever
74 songs from the movies: Almost Paradise • Chariots of Fire • My Heart Will Go On • Take My Breath Away • Unchained Melody • You'll Be in My Heart • more.
00310063...$19.95

The Best R&B Songs Ever
66 songs, including: Baby Love • Endless Love • Here and Now • I Will Survive • Saving All My Love for You • Stand By Me • What's Going On • and more.
00310184...$19.95

The Best Rock Songs Ever
Over 60 songs: All Shook Up • Blue Suede Shoes • Born to Be Wild • Every Breath You Take • Free Bird • Hey Jude • We Got the Beat • Wild Thing • more!
00490424...$18.95

The Best Songs Ever
Over 70 must-own classics, including: All I Ask of You • Crazy • Edelweiss • Love Me Tender • Memory • My Funny Valentine • Tears in Heaven • Unforgettable • The Way We Were • A Whole New World • and more.
00359224...$22.95

More of the Best Songs Ever
79 more favorites: April in Paris • Candle in the Wind • Endless Love • Misty • My Blue Heaven • My Heart Will Go On • Stella by Starlight • Witchcraft • more.
00310437...$19.95

The Best Standards Ever, Vol. 1 (A-L)
72 beautiful ballads, including: All the Things You Are • Bewitched • Getting to Know You • God Bless' the Child • Hello, Young Lovers • It's Only a Paper Moon • I've Got You Under My Skin • The Lady Is a Tramp.
00359231...$15.95

The Best Standards Ever, Vol. 2 (M-Z)
72 songs, including: Makin' Whoopee • Misty • Moonlight in Vermont • My Funny Valentine • People Will Say We're in Love • Smoke Gets in Your Eyes • Strangers in the Night • Tuxedo Junction • Yesterday.
00359232...$15.95

More of the Best Standards Ever, Vol. 1 (A-L)
76 all-time favorites, including: Ain't Misbehavin' • Always • Autumn in New York • Body and Soul • Desafinado • Fever • Fly Me to the Moon • For All We Know • Georgia on My Mind • Lazy River • and more.
00310813...$17.95

More of the Best Standards Ever, Vol. 2 (M-Z)
75 more stunning standards: Mona Lisa • Mood Indigo • Moon River • My Favorite Things • Norwegian Wood • Route 66 • Sentimental Journey • Stella by Starlight • What a Diff'rence a Day Made • What'll I Do? • You Are the Sunshine of My Life • more.
00310814...$17.95

FOR MORE INFORMATION, SEE YOUR LOCAL MUSIC DEALER, OR WRITE TO:

HAL•LEONARD CORPORATION
7777 W. BLUEMOUND RD. P.O. BOX 13819 MILWAUKEE, WI 53213

Visit us on-line for complete songlists.
www.halleonard.com

Prices, contents and availability subject to change without notice. Not all products available outside the U.S.A.

1002

Contemporary Classics

Your favorite songs for piano, voice and guitar.

The Definitive Rock 'n' Roll Collection

A classic collection of the best songs from the early rock 'n' roll years – 1955-1966. 97 songs, including: Barbara Ann • Chantilly Lace • Dream Lover • Duke of Earl • Earth Angel • Great Balls of Fire • Louie, Louie • Rock Around the Clock • Ruby Baby • Runaway • (Seven Little Girls) Sitting in the Back Seat • Stay • Surfin' U.S.A. • Wild Thing • Woolly Bully • and more.
00490195 ....$29.95

The Big Book of Rock

78 of rock's biggest hits, including: Addicted to Love • American Pie • Born to Be Wild • Cold As Ice • Dust in the Wind • Free Bird • Goodbye Yellow Brick Road • Groovin' • Hey Jude • I Love Rock 'N' Roll • Lay Down Sally • Layla • Livin' on a Prayer • Louie Louie • Maggie May • Me and Bobby McGee • Monday, Monday • Owner of a Lonely Heart • Shout • Walk This Way • We Didn't Start the Fire • You Really Got Me • and more.
00311566...$19.95

Big Book of Movie Music

Features 73 classic songs from 72 movies: Beauty and the Beast • Change the World • Eye of the Tiger • I Finally Found Someone • The John Dunbar Theme • Somewhere in Time • Stayin' Alive • Take My Breath Away • Unchained Melody • The Way You Look Tonight • You've Got a Friend in Me • Zorro's Theme • more.
00311582 ....$19.95

The Best Rock Songs Ever

70 of the best rock songs from yesterday and today, including: All Day and All of the Night • All Shook Up • Blue Suede Shoes • Born to Be Wild • Boys Are Back in Town • Every Breath You Take • Faith • Free Bird • Hey Jude • I Still Haven't Found What I'm Looking For • Livin' on a Prayer • Lola • Louie Louie • Maggie May • Money • (She's) Some Kind of Wonderful • Takin' Care of Business • Walk This Way • We Didn't Start the Fire • We Got the Beat • Wild Thing • more!
00490424 ....$18.95

Contemporary Vocal Groups

This exciting new collection includes 35 huge hits by 18 of today's best vocal groups, including 98 Degrees, TLC, Destiny's Child, Savage Garden, Boyz II Men, Dixie Chicks, 'N Sync, and more! Songs include: Bills, Bills, Bills • Bug a Boo • Diggin' on You • The Hardest Thing • I'll Make Love to You • In the Still of the Nite (I'll Remember) • Ready to Run • Tearin' Up My Heart • Truly, Madly, Deeply • Waterfalls • Wide Open Spaces • and more.
00310605 ....$14.95

Motown Anthology

This songbook commemorates Motown's 40th Anniversary with 68 songs, background information on this famous record label, and lots of photos. Songs include: ABC • Baby Love • Ben • Dancing in the Street • Easy • For Once in My Life • My Girl • Shop Around • The Tracks of My Tears • War • What's Going On • You Can't Hurry Love • and many more.
00310367 ....$19.95

Best Contemporary Ballads

Includes 35 favorites: And So It Goes • Angel • Beautiful in My Eyes • Don't Know Much • Fields of Gold • Hero • I Will Remember You • Iris • My Heart Will Go On • Tears in Heaven • Valentine • You Were Meant for Me • You'll Be in My Heart • and more.
00310583 ....$16.95

Contemporary Hits

Contains 35 favorites by artists such as Sarah McLachlan, Whitney Houston, 'N Sync, Mariah Carey, Christina Aguilera, Celine Dion, and other top stars. Songs include: Adia • Building a Mystery • The Hardest Thing • I Believe in You and Me • I Drive Myself Crazy • I'll Be • Kiss Me • My Father's Eyes • Reflection • Smooth • Torn • and more!
00310589...$16.95

Jock Rock Hits

32 stadium-shaking favorites, including: Another One Bites the Dust • The Boys Are Back in Town • Freeze-Frame • Gonna Make You Sweat (Everybody Dance Now) • I Got You (I Feel Good) • Na Na Hey Hey Kiss Him Goodbye • Rock & Roll – Part II (The Hey Song) • Shout • Tequila • We Are the Champions • We Will Rock You • Whoomp! (There It Is) • Wild Thing • and more.
00310105...$14.95

Rock Ballads

31 sentimental favorites, including: All for Love • Bed of Roses • Dust in the Wind • Everybody Hurts • Right Here Waiting • Tears in Heaven • and more.
00311673...$14.95

FOR MORE INFORMATION, SEE YOUR LOCAL MUSIC DEALER, OR WRITE TO:

HAL•LEONARD®
CORPORATION

7777 W. BLUEMOUND RD. P.O. BOX 13819 MILWAUKEE, WI 53213

Visit Hal Leonard Online at www.halleonard.com

Prices, contents & availability subject to change without notice.